Affirmative Action

Affirmative Action

From A Caribbean's Perspective

Patricia Ferdinand, Ph.D.

Library of Congress Control Number:		2014910076
ISBN:	Hardcover	978-1-4990-2429-6
	Softcover	978-1-4990-2440-1
	eBook	978-1-4990-2425-8

This book was printed in the United States of America.

Rev. date: 08/18/2014

To order additional copies of this book, contact:
Xlibris LLC
1-888-795-4274
www.Xlibris.com
Orders@Xlibris.com
618284

I want to dedicate this book to my children Andree and Michelle and grandchildren Ezra, Esther, and Ezekiel. Thanking God for sustaining Esther Grace who was diagnosed with a terminal illness in 2010.

AFFIRMATIVE ACTION FROM A CARIBBEAN'S PERSPECTIVE

"Grandma! Open your eyes! The sun is up! Please open your eyes, Grandma, the sun is up! Please, Grandma, come and read for me."

"Zeke, Grandma is sleeping," says Grandma.

"*Please*, Grandma, please come and read for me."

"Okay, Zeke, bring me the book," says Grandma.

Zeke brings three to four books for Grandma to read in the early morning.

"Hop on Pop. Up, pup! Pup is up.

House Mouse! Mouse on house!

Mouse house! House on mouse."

After a while, Zeke exclaims, "Grandma, I want eggs, Grandma!"

"Eggs, Zeke?"

"Yes, Grandma, boiled eggs!"

Grandma goes downstairs and boils six eggs.

"Grandma, I would like two eggs, and I want to peel the shell off myself."said Zeke.

"Please, Grandma, I also want sausage with my eggs!"

"Okay, Zeke, sausage with your eggs is coming up," says Grandma.

"Grandma, I need milk with my eggs," says Esther.

"Grandma, how about my cereal?" says Ezra.

"Cereal coming up," says Grandma.

"Grandma! Grandma! Please come and play house with me, Grandma."

"Essie, you will have to finish eating before we play house," says Grandma.

"But I want to cook some breakfast for you, Grandma."

"Okay, Essie, we will play house after you are done eating."

At about 11:30 a.m. as the day rolls on, it is sleep time for Zeke and Essie.

"Time to sleep," says Grandma.

"I do not want to sleep, Grandma," says Zeke.

"Yes you do," says Grandma.

Grandma picks Zeke up in her arms and begins to sing,

> Pretty painted butterfly
> What do you do all day?
> I roam about the sunny field,
> Nothing to do but play.
> Nothing to do but play
> All the live long day;
> Fly butterfly, fly butterfly
> Don't waste your time away.

Before long, Zeke's eyes close shut and Grandma puts both Essie and Zeke to sleep.

Now Grandma gets a chance to spend some quality time with Ezra.

"Ezra, how would you like to spend some time with Grandma?" asked Grandma.

"I want to shoot some basketball hoops with you, Grandma."

"Okay, let's go outside in the back and play."

Poor Grandma puts on her sneakers and goes outside with Ezra to shoot hoops.

"Ezra, let's have a little competition. Let see how many baskets we can get if we stand outside the line."

"Okay, Grandma."

"See, Ezra, the best way to improve is to practice your skills. You have to practice, practice, and practice. You have to practice reading, practice your pieces on the piano, practice your math problems that you get for homework. Practice makes perfect, Ezra. That is the best way to excel, Ezra. That is what Mama G, your great-grandmother, taught me when I was growing up."

"Okay, Grandma."

My Mother (Mama G)

My mother, Eglantine Buchannan, born in 1916, was the oldest of the children born to Florence Stewart. Her father was Jabes Buchannan, who traveled back and forth from Cuba to Jamaica.

"So, Mom, why did he travel so much from Cuba to Jamaica? What was his occupation?" I asked.

"I really do not know what he did. He was a businessman and was wealthy because he owned horses, cows and goats." She replied.

Jabes was married to Ms. Currant Buchannan, a church organist. She had no children, and so she agreed to raise my mother, whom Jabes had out of wedlock with Florence Stewart. My mother was four years old when she left her mother to go and live with Ms. Currant Buchannan in Redbrook, Riverside, Jamaica.

Ms. Currant raised my mother "to be a lady." That meant that she was taught to keep house, be a good wife, and do wifely duties such as cook, clean, darn clothes, and please her husband by being a gracious and submissive wife.

My mother was also educated. She attended Roseau's High School and later went to Bethlehem Teacher's College. Ms. Currant also taught my mother to play the piano.

Soon after my mother graduated from teacher's college, her father died.

"Mother, what was the cause of your father's death?"

"I do not know," she replied. "I just know that I inherited land which was sold to help pay for my college tuition."

About three years later, my mother moved to Goodwill, Hanover, and, soon after, married my father, Rupert Gordon, a very handsome, charming mulatto who was a soldier in the Jamaican Army.

Being in the army in those days was a status symbol. My father was a proud soldier and loved dressing up in his uniform. He was stationed in Kingston, Jamaica, and would travel to Goodwill to be with my mother whenever he got leave. My father was also a child born out of wedlock. His mother was of Irish descent and his father, Carlton Gordon, was the son of an upper-class white family in Montego Bay, Jamaica.

Rupert and Eglantine had three girls. The first child, Yvonne, was born in 1945; I was born in 1947; and my younger sister, Rosemarie Etta, was born July 1951.

"I was the apple of my father's eye," she said. Whenever I arrived home from college, I would receive a sample of all that he and Ms. Currant had eaten for that day. They were a very loving couple who impressed upon her the value of getting a good education.

Jabes would say, "No one can take from you that which you have stored up in your brain, so you must go and get that little piece of paper."

My mother passed these same values unto her three girls. They resound like a record in my ear. "You must go and get that little piece of paper." Of course she was referring to our achieving some type of diploma or degree from a university.

My mother also insisted that we should strive to get an education because as girls, we needed to be independent and not have to depend on a man for support. She used to say, "When you get married, you will always be able to leave your husband if you are not happy because you will be able to earn for yourself."

My mother was an elementary school teacher. She was also my most important teacher. She helped us with homework during schooltime and taught us during the summers when we were on vacation.

Her role as a teacher extended to her grandchildren. She would come and spend a month each summer. Her responsibility then was to teach the children to read. She taught my two children, Michelle and Andree, to read, and all my nieces and nephews.

When I went to school, the teachers, including my mother, used corporal punishment to make us learn. Nevertheless, we as students during the time we were growing up did not regard this as physical abuse. For me, I was so afraid of punishment that I tried my best to perform well.

Over the years, my mother has been a tremendous source of support for our family. In 1979, while I was working on my doctorate degree, my mother came to reside with my family for two years. My oldest daughter, Michelle, was already five years old. My daughter Michelle became the benefactor of my mother's tutelage and her positive influence.

When Michael, my sister's older son, was studying for his medical boards, my mother traveled to Gainesville, Florida, and lived with Michael for two weeks while he studied for his medical boards. During this time, she cooked, cleaned, and ministered to him spiritually by prayer and reading the Bible.

My mother was also a source of spiritual strength. She learned this from her stepmother, Ms. Currant Buchannan, who was a devoted Christian. She taught us to love and respect the elderly, to be humble, and to have self-confidence and self-respect.

My Elementary Schoolteachers (1954)

I will never forget my third-grade teacher Mrs. Robinson, and my fourth-grade teacher Ms. Dick. These were teachers at the same school where my mother taught, Woodsley Primary School in Kingston, Jamaica.

Since I was the child of one of the teachers, I was subjected to much more scrutiny than the average child. They had more expectations of me.

Ms. Robinson was a tall heavyset woman who wore her glasses far down on her nose. She was famous for beating the children with a strap over their backs. I feared her with a passion and figured out that the best thing to do was to be on her good side by paying careful attention to my work.

Ms. Dick was this tall, ugly lady with a wart on her nose. One day she gave us some arithmetic problems to do. She said, "Please take time to do these problems correctly." I hastily did my problems and finished first in the class. Consequently, some of them were incorrect. Ms. Dick was mad. She sent one of the students outside in the yard to pick what we called a switch (a branch from a tamarind tree). She was going to beat me with the switch. I created such a big ruckus in the class that Ms. Robinson, who was nearby, came and rescued me from getting the beating.

A year later, I left Woodley Primary School and was accepted into a very prestigious elementary school called St. George's Girls' School. The principal here was a short upper-class mulatto lady named Ms. McPherson. She also was a terror to us, and everyone feared her.

When I got to the fifth grade, my mother wanted me to sit for the common entrance examination so that I would earn a scholarship to attend high school, which is equivalent to the middle school in the United States. Therefore, after a year at St. George's Girls', I was removed and placed at a small private school, which was individually owned by one Mrs. Patterson. This was called Patterson's Preparatory School.

Mrs. Patterson was tall and heavyset with rolling big eyes. She combed her hair so that she appeared to have horns in her head. Because she smoked, she had a raspy voice that made her seem to roar. Ma Pete, as she was called, had only a few dresses. Students believed that when she wore a certain dress, she would be on the warpath.

Ma Pete was my mother's friend, so she kept keen eyes on me. Every week we were given a list of spelling words to learn. On Monday mornings bright and early, we would have a spelling test. Ma Pete would stand out front and call out the words one at a time to the fourth-, fifth-, and sixth-grade classes. More than three words incorrectly spelled were rewarded by lashes with a strap. Since I was terribly afraid of lashes, I was careful to study my spelling words along with their definitions. When we got arithmetic problems to do, I would try to get help from one of my classmates so I could avoid Ma Pete's wrath. I sat the common entrance at Ma Pete's school and was successful in winning a scholarship to Arlenne High School.

Arlenne High School (1959–1965)

This school was founded by American Missionaries Rev. John Pearson and Mary Pearson, who were associated with the Church of God denomination in Jamaica. They had a daughter, also named Mary Pearson, who was the principal of the school when I started there.

Mary Pearson was extremely eccentric and always spoke with a very loud voice. She had an ugly grin. When she smiled, she would show her ugly teeth, which seemed that they had not been cleaned for months. She drove a small model Prefect, and one could always know when Mary was coming up the road that led to the school because Mary would ride the clutch whenever she had to change gears.

Our school had an enrollment of about three hundred children. Ms. Mary, as she was called, had a way of keeping us quiet when she walked through the halls of the school. She would walk around with her fingers on her lips and say, "Stop it."

On occasion, whenever the algebra teacher was absent, she would be the substitute teacher. She was most comical as she tried to explain certain equations in algebra. She made up stories about the "A family and the B family." As she spoke, she would flash a wide grimace across her face and show her ugly teeth. Simultaneously the saliva from her cheeks would settle in the corner of her lips and create an unpleasant sight.

She said, "The A family had to cross the fence [which was the equal sign]. When the A family crossed the fence, their clothes got torn and so they were changed." This meant that when the characters on the left of the equal sign got moved to the right, the sign would change from positive to negative or vice-versa. Although this was her weird way of explaining things, we really did learn algebra when Ms. Mary taught us.

I was eleven years old when I started attending Arlenne High School. My older sister Yvonne had already been in attendance there for two years. My favorite subjects then were art and biology. My favorite teachers were my biology teachers because they made learning fun. I believe that I learned very early to associate math with spankings and always approached it with fear and uncertainty.

My first biology teacher was a pretty, young, slender, and fashionable black female named Ms. Wiggins. I remember she would take us on nature walks to collect specimens of leaves so we could study the different leaf formations. When we studied seeds, we would walk around the campus, which was acres wide, and collect the different fruits with their seeds and discuss them. Our biology laboratory was outdoors. We studied the different kinds of roots. We caught our own animals and studied all their parts.

In the second form of high school, I had a young male teacher who was tall, dark, and handsome. He had large bulging eyes. When he rolled them he was very inspiring. Mr. Campbell was smart and very assertive and always nicely dressed. He came to Arlenne soon after he had graduated from the University of the West Indies with a degree in zoology and botany.

This teacher made a very positive impression on me. This caused me to want to learn everything that I could in biology. After school each day, I would go home and take my older sister's biology notes, put them together with mine, and study them.

Clearly, my love for the subject of biology was definitely associated with the love and admiration I had for my teachers. They were tremendous positive role models in my academic life. I am very cognizant of this fact, and so I always try to appear as attractive as possible when I lecture to my students today.

When I got to the more senior classes, I had a wonderful, inspiring teacher. Her name was Mrs. Ivy Townsend, who did her graduate work in the United States. It was this teacher who motivated me to do independent research. She taught me how to do very intricate detailed dissections and insisted that we made drawings of our dissections of animals. We spent hours dissecting earthworms, cockroaches, dogfish, frogs, and guinea pigs.

In Jamaica we had to catch our own frogs. My classmates and I would go to the reservoirs where it was damp, look under rocks, and catch the frogs that would be hiding there. They were not injected with colored latex. We had to be very meticulous so that we would not cut blood vessels and cause excessive bleeding.

Mrs. Townsend seemed to be always available to help. She kept the laboratory open all day so we could come in during our free time and work. During the time we spent with her, she would encourage us to read scientific articles from Scientific American magazines. My thirst for learning biology became more intense and I began to read everything I could find that was related to biology.

I had two other male teachers, Mr. Ramsey and Mr. Roberts, who also mentored me and encouraged me to read immensely. It was Mr. Ramsey who recommended to my parents that I should be given the opportunity to attend the Center for Democratic Education in Berkeley, California.

1960–1963 in America
Center for Democratic Education, 1963

In the summer of 1963, I was chosen to attend a summer program, the Center for Democratic Education in Berkeley, California, along with two other Jamaican girls, Thelma Blackburne and Marlene Green. Thelma and I attended Arlenne High School, a private school founded by American Missionaries.

The main focus at Arlenne High School was our religious education and academic preparation for British examinations. Jamaica at that time was still a British colony, and so we had to take British qualifying examinations that gained us entry into a British university.

In high school, we were taught British history, and not much attention was paid to what was going on in America. In fact, we were always given the impression that the British education was superior to the American education.

When I was in school, slavery was not presented as a bad thing. As kids we seemed to boast about the fact that our forefathers were slaves. Now we arrived in the United States and were presented with the horrors of slavery and the inequalities suffered by people of color in America.

Our lack of awareness and exposure to the racial issues in the '60s stemmed from the fact that there was no television on the island of Jamaica. Maybe a few rich folks had some sort of TV, but television had not come to the island during the time that I grew up in Jamaica. All we had access to was the radio. I remember that we would listen intently to the fights of Floyd Patterson and Sonny Liston. Everyone cheered for Floyd Patterson and did not want Sonny Liston to beat him. However, the time came when in one minute, Patterson was knocked down by Sonny Liston. We listened to cricket on radio. Of course we went to the movies, and at that time, my child idol was Elvis Presley. I remember when Nat King Cole came to Jamaica we all worshipped these idols but were never embroiled in racial issues.

In the 1960s, there was a television in almost every America living room. This was not the case on the island of Jamaica. Consequently, Jamaicans young and old were protected from the adverse effects of prejudice in culture and politics. We were protected from the constant bombardment with images of war and depression associated with racism.

The opportunity to travel to the United States of America and spend a summer on the beautiful campus of Berkeley University was tremendous. We were there to attend the Center for Democratic Education. The diversity of the campers was amazing. We had one fellow there from an Indian reservation, Charlie, who was always a little strange in his behavior. There were about six African Americans, and the majority of the others were white Americans. This composition made for lively discussion because many of us were being exposed to individuals from various cultures for the first time and also individuals of varied opinions. Daily we had lively discussions about how we viewed racism in each culture. We took trips to the inner city and were guided by a black American counselor named Villel, who was soft-spoken and gentle and graciously guided our tours of the black ghettos in Oakland, California.

This exposure was a terrific attempt to ideally educate young minds about the racial divide in America.

However, it was difficult for me to identify with the severity and seriousness of the racial divide in America at that time. One summer was certainly not enough although it was a noble attempt to change one's thinking.

1960–1965

In March 1961, President F. Kennedy issued Executive Order 10925, which created the Committee on Equal Employment Opportunity and mandated that projects financed with federal funds "take affirmative action" to ensure that hiring and employment practices are free of racial bias.

On July 2, 1964, President Lyndon Johnson signed the Civil Rights Act that prohibits discrimination of all kinds based on race, color, religion, and national origin. In September 24, 1965, he signed Executive Order 11246 enforcing affirmative action, compelling federal contractors to establish written programs. President Johnson elaborated on the importance of affirmative action to achieving true freedom for African Americans.

In 1965, I graduated from high school and obtained a job at the Kingston Mutual Building Society.

The general manager at this time was Mr. George Harris, who was one of the elders in the Church of God, which was affiliated with Arlenne High School, which I attended. He was faithful to recruit students who were outstanding graduates, and so I was one of them.

It was here that I met many other young people who had their mind set on going to universities abroad. My knowledge of universities in the United States was very limited. My first exposure to one was when I attended the summer camp at Berkeley University. Also on my way back from California, I stopped in New York City to visit my uncle Ronald and his wife, Earnestine, and had the opportunity to visit Columbia University.

My uncle Ron was a Jamaican athlete who received an athletic scholarship to study at the University of Arkansas at Pine Bluff. He married Earnestine, a native of Arkansas. After they both graduated from college they moved to New York City where they were raising a family. Both my uncle and his wife, Earnestine, worked at Columbia University as research technicians. He worked in a chemistry laboratory because he had gained a bachelor of science degree in chemistry and she a bachelor of science in biology.

Since the time I was in high school, my uncle took a keen interest in my academic progress. While he was in college, he would write and give me all kinds of incentives to do well. Soon after I arrived in New York he invited me to visit the campus of Columbia University. When I got to the laboratory where he worked, he dressed me in a white laboratory coat and took me around to meet his coworkers.

This was a great feeling, walking around in a white laboratory coat. The only people that I knew at that time who wore white laboratory coats were doctors. My dream of becoming a medical doctor had come to pass just from the feeling. My uncle was my role model and mentor and encouraged me greatly to apply for admission to Columbia University.

It was at Kingston Mutual Building Society that I became more encouraged to apply for admission to an American university. While there, I met other smart young people who had graduated from some of the most prestigious private high schools. Their sights were set on going to college in America.

My friends Faylene and Kay were graduates of St. Thomas High School. They were from upper-middle-class families. Dorman, another dear friend, was a graduate of Jamaica College, another prestigious boys' high school. These friends of mine were always preoccupied with the thought of going to college, and since I spent a lot of my time in their company, I was greatly influenced by them.

There is a saying in Jamaica that says, "Show me your friends and I will tell you who you are." If I had no plans of going to an American university before, just hanging out with these individuals changed my thinking and ambitions, although I did not know how I was going to afford the college tuition.

My mother at that time was going through a very difficult married relationship. She did all that she could to provide for me and my other two sisters. She sent us all to private school, but she did not have the means to encourage me to attend a college abroad.

During the time I spent with my friends Kay, Faylene, and Dorman, I learned that if I wanted to gain admission to an American university, I would have to take the Scholastic Aptitude Test (SAT). I knew nothing about this exam. No one at the school I attended ever mentioned that I needed to prepare for this examination, the reason being that Jamaica was a British colony during the time I went to school. We were always prepared to take British examinations and directed to attend British universities. In addition, we were also given the impression that an American education was inferior to the British education. Our teachers always encouraged us to go to England to study or to Canada.

In addition, my father at that time was employed at the University of the West Indies (UWI) in Mona Heights, Jamaica, and so I was encouraged by many to apply for admission at UWI. Nevertheless, since my friends were going to take the SAT exam, I agreed to take it also. I was not prepared, did not prepare, and consequently I am sure I was at a disadvantage going into this examination.

Reflecting on my life thus far, I think that I had been given all the tools that I needed to succeed in college, whether in America, England, or Jamaica. Like a tender plant, I had been nurtured by caring teachers. I was exposed to a great deal of extracurricular activity such as playing the piano, elocution, and singing in the school choir and on radio in Jamaica. I was an outstanding athlete and graduated at the top of my class. I had proven myself as a leader and was the president of the student body, captain of my sports team, president of the student's Christian movement, and a very devout believer in the Christian faith.

My high school emphasized strong religious principles. However, it was not equipped with the scientific laboratories that would allow me to compete in an American school alongside brilliant students from science high schools such as Stuyvesant, Bronx High School of Science. I did not realize my lack of preparation for attendance at one of the best universities in America. Or did I?

I applied to UWI and two American universities. Despite the fact that I did not know my SAT scores, I was accepted to the University of the West Indies at Mona and one of the American universities in New York City.

Summer 1966

In the summer of 1966 my uncle, his family, and I flew from Montego Bay, Jamaica, into Miami Airport. From there we picked up our car and set out on our journey to New York City.

I was very quiet and pensive during this long journey. I had taken along with me my faith-based books in addition to a copy of the Bible. I kept thinking that although I did not have all the tuition for school, my faithful God would supply all my needs. He would make a way.

As we were passing through North Carolina, I asked my uncle to stop and allow me to use the restroom. He did not share with me his apprehension but stopped at a small pub so I could ask permission to use their restroom. I was not aware of the racial divide at that time in America and did not have any reason for concern or any hesitation to make my request.

"Ron!" my aunt exclaimed. "Are you sure they are going to allow her to use the toilet?"

"Why not let her try?" my uncle responded. So I went in and was allowed to use the restroom.

There is a saying, "When ignorance is bliss, it is folly to resist." So my ignorance prevailed, and I was able to relieve my bladder for the rest of our journey.

The sixties in America were also the height of the Hippie Era. The drug of choice was heroin and LSD. I was raised in such a sheltered environment in Jamaica that I knew nothing about the drug culture. The only drug I knew about was the Jamaican ganga called marijuana in America. I knew that this was something the members of the Rastafarian cult smoked that we believed made them violent.

Members of the Rastafarian cult in Jamaica before the sixties were outcasts of our society. Any family member who joined the Rastafarian cult in the '60s would be disowned and considered dead.

The hippie culture was popular in the sixties and gained notoriety during the civil rights movements through freedom songs sung by artists such as Joan Baez; Peter, Paul, and Mary; Bob Dillon and Pete Seeger. I loved the folk songs sung by these artists. They were introduced to me when I attended the Center for Democratic Education in Berkeley, California, in 1963. I learned to play the guitar and would sing many of these freedom songs. Songs like "If you miss the train I am on, you will know that I am gone."

I guess that singing these freedom songs did expose me to certain elements of the hippie culture. Because when I arrived in Washington Square Park in 1966, I would see the hippies in the streets and on the sidewalks sitting idly by strumming on their guitars and playing these songs.

During this time America was deeply involved in the Vietnam War. In February 1965, President Johnson began the air war, ordering sustained bombing on North Vietnam. He also sent the first ground troops to South Vietnam. A month later, faculty at the University of Michigan organized an SDS-supported teach-in at Ann Arbor. In April, the first major national antiwar demonstration, organized by the Students for a Democratic Society, took place in Washington. The nation became divided by the war and peace protests occurring at many universities including New York University.

I arrived during the time of heated expressions of disapproval of America's involvement in Vietnam. This was also the time when there was a draft of young men. I realized this because many of my classmates were young men who in order to avoid the draft enrolled in college.

It was at this very exciting time that I arrived in New York City to be enrolled in college as a biology major. Growing up in Jamaica I had never participated in any demonstrations, and so for me being surrounded by this climate of revolt was new to me. I also was not accustomed to traveling by subway. I lived in Queens Long Island with my uncle and his family. In order to get to Washington Square in Manhattan, I was going to have to take a bus and the subway to the city. My uncle was very willing to accompany me on the subway at the beginning so that I would get accustomed to riding on the subway.

Registration time came, and I went alone to do this. I still had no idea how my tuition was going to be paid. My faith in God allowed me to move forward despite my uncertainties. When I arrived at the registrar's office, I was informed that my file was incomplete. In addition to a few other things, I needed a photograph to be attached. The registrar instructed me to "go downstairs to the five-and-dime store" and I would be able to get one. I had never heard the term "five and dime" before; nevertheless, I set out to find one. Turns out this was at the time a Woolworth store. The Woolworth store had come to Jamaica a few years before I left for the United States, but it was never referred to as "five and dime."

Another frustration for me was my awkwardness in using a map for directions around campus. In Jamaica during my time no one used a map to get around town. We either knew where we were going or we did not. In my sheltered upbringing, I took the bus or walked to school, work, or church and back home. My map skills were limited to the study of geography. Using a map to find my way around campus was a major task and very frustrating. I spent many days and hours just crying because everything was so new and different and I was all alone trying to navigate my way in New York City.

Another thing I needed to complete my application was a health examination. Again I was instructed that I could go to First Avenue and Twenty-Third Street to have this done. The office of the registrar was located in the main building located at University and Waverly Place. I had become familiar with Fifth Avenue and figured out that First Avenue would only be four blocks away, and so I began to walk. I walked and walked but there was no First Avenue in sight. On my way, I saw some workmen in the street and enquired of them how many more blocks I needed to walk. They instructed me that before I came to First Ave I would have to cross Lexington Ave, Madison, Park, Third, Second, and then First. What they failed to tell me was that these were extremely long blocks. I had done some walking in Jamaica as a schoolgirl but in those days I walked with a group of friends, and together we chatted and played along the way, but now I was walking alone on the streets of New York City for the first time.

Soon after these problems were solved, I was then confronted with my tuition payment by the bursar. One day after my application was complete, I accidentally walked into a room where registration was taking place and I found a leaflet about a tuition payment plan. I took this leaflet home to my uncle, and he immediately agreed to cosign for me to participate in this plan so my tuition would be paid.

The next problem that arose was that in order to pay my tuition monthly, I needed a job. My uncle said, "Earnestine and I will provide you with food and shelter, but you will have to find a job to make these monthly payments."

"That will be fine with me," I said. "I will take this signed application to the college tomorrow and then look about finding a job." Again my naivety kicked in because I did not realize that I was committing to going to school full-time and working full-time. In addition, I had a very long commute. I lived in Springfield Gardens Queens and had to travel back and forth to College in Manhattan. This was like a two-hour commute each day. Then there was the fact that I was on a student visa and did not have permission to work. However, most New Yorkers did not know much about a green card in the sixties, and so it was not very difficult to pick up odd jobs. The problem was that I went to school full-time during the day and then worked at night usually doing filing for some type of small company. I would fall asleep doing the filing and so frequently got fired for the mistakes I made.

About the beginning of my second year, a cousin of mine who worked for Lugoff Theaters was able to get me a job as an usher at the Fifth Avenue Cinema. This was located on Fifth Avenue and Thirteenth Street in the West Village nearby where I went to school. Today the Parson's School of Design is located in this building.

For me this was a convenient location because as soon I was finished with my classes, I was able to walk to work. I worked for Lugoff Theaters for the remainder of my time in college. My hours of employment were from 5:00 p.m. to 11:00 p.m.

I tell this story because it is important to factor it into my recruitment as a black student who fulfilled the requirement of affirmative action. Here I was a full-time student in college working full-time and trying to compete with my other classmates, the majority of whom lived in the dormitories and did not have to work. I think of two of my very good friends; one was Rachael Grant whose father was the attorney general of Liberia. She was rolling in money and certainly did not have to work. Then there was Maria Lepada, a Greek girl whose sister was a doctor. She lived in the dormitories and did not have to work. Yet we were all premedical majors competing in the same classes.

The job of an usher at the Lugoff Theaters at that time in the '60s was not only to usher guests to their seats but also we had to brew coffee and serve it in demitasse cups. No sitting down was allowed. We wore black and had to be extremely polite and hospitable. Some of our clientele were people like Dustin Hoffman and other celebrities who lived in the village.

My First Year as a Student
in College (1966)

Since I was totally unfamiliar with the American system, I really was at a complete disadvantage starting out for college. I fell into the trap of allowing advisors to design my academic program without really knowing my personal financial circumstance.

As a first-year biology major in the premed program, I was given for the first semester general biology, general chemistry, calculus, and classics. In Jamaica, I was only exposed to British literature and European history. We had to memorize massive excerpts of Shakespeare but never read any classics. I only did algebra, no calculus, and very little chemistry.

I remember my general chemistry professor, Dr. Myron Whensaw, who was very impatient and tolerated very few questions in lectures. People like me who had very little chemistry were lost.

I was fortunate to have done an enormous amount of biology. I had taken the equivalent of advance placement biology, and so I really did not have to spend a lot of time studying biology and still maintained a B average in all my courses.

To make matters worse, I also registered for beginner's French along with my other courses. I had taken five years of Spanish and Latin and so wanted to learn another language. With very little time to study since I spent so much time working and traveling, I began to struggle with French. To make matters worse, most of the testing was done in the language laboratory using audio equipment. It made no difference how much I studied; I just could not hear and understand the questions. I related this to my professor, and he seemed to empathize. He would say, "Do not worry, you will be OK. "Of course I was not OK because I ended up with my only F grade on my undergraduate transcript. My first year in college was a total disaster. I surely was at a disadvantage.

I had come from a small high school in Jamaica with about three hundred students. In each of my classes there were about fifteen to twenty students. At school I was sitting in lectures, especially the science classes, with approximately three hundred students. My biology classmates were loud and boisterous. There were many men who were enrolled, and it was clear that they needed to be in college to avoid the draft. They would walk through the hallways and their loud, boisterous voices would be quite troubling to me.

Because I did not live on campus or in the dorms, I had very few friends in my first year. Most of my friends were people from the church I attended. They were my extended family, and they were caring and encouraging.

In my second year, I made a friend named Hugh. He was from Trinidad. He reminded me that before long, I would learn how to make an A grade in my courses

"Once you learn how much effort you need to put in to make an A grade, you will keep making As." This was absolutely true and worked for me.

This philosophy is true even today. I taught my daughters this principle, the principle of striving for perfection. I once met a flautist who aspired to getting a position in the New York Philharmonic Orchestra. She told me that she had auditioned many times for a place in the orchestra but was never successful though she was an excellent flautist. My question to her was "How could someone such as yourself with such excellent skills not be able to do this?"

Her answer was "There are many excellent musicians competing for a position in the orchestra. It is the individual who makes absolutely no errors in the audition who will eventually be chosen."

The same principle holds in the acting, music, and sports arena. The people at the top of their game are mostly error-free. This principle became a reality for me as I matured in life and professionally. Little by little I learned to achieve perfection in school. Attaining perfection made a difference between an A grade and a B grade. It meant studying and knowing my material thoroughly. It meant knowing everything and not just some things. It meant spending extra time to know. It meant collaborating and working with my classmates who were willing to work with me. By the help of God, I began to overcome my so-called disadvantage.

"During a panel discussion at Harvard University's reunion for African American alumni in 2003–2005, two prominent black professors at the institution—Lani Guinier and Henry Louis Gates—pointed out an unintended effect of affirmative action policies at Harvard. They stated that only about one third of black Harvard undergraduates were from families in which all four grandparents were born into African American communities. The majority of black students at Harvard were Caribbean and African immigrants."

In my freshman biology class at the College of Arts and Sciences in 1966, the demographics were as follows for the black students:

- One girl was from Liberia.

- One girl was African American.

- Two men were from Haiti.

- One girl was from Panama.

- One girl from Jamaica.

Across the board in 1966, there were two other men from Liberia, two from South Africa who were not science majors, two other Jamaican girls who went to high school in Jamaica, and we would see a couple other students who were African American. We would pass each other in the streets as we went from class to class.

So yes, I agree that the schools did go abroad to recruit black students to fill their quota. Were we disadvantaged? Many of the foreign students especially those from African countries were not financially disadvantaged. I know for a fact that my best friend from Liberia was the daughter of the attorney general in Liberia at that time. She lived in the dorm and attended boarding high school in the United States.

I speak for myself and all the other Jamaican students and say that financially we struggled to pay tuition. We had to work full-time and go to college full-time. Since we could not afford to live in the dormitories, we also had to travel from neighboring communities. Consequently, we had very limited study time that would enable us to compete effectively.

For myself, I also was at a disadvantage academically. Here I was enrolled in the premedical program. I had very little preparation in chemistry, physics, and mathematics.

Except for the last two years at Arlenne High, we had no chemistry or physics laboratories. Our biology laboratories were mostly outdoors. Nevertheless, my preparation in biology was outstanding.

Very few of our science teachers and mathematics teachers were university graduates. Many attended what was called teacher's college, a three-year program, and consequently, their preparation for teaching science and mathematics was limited.

In the first semester of my freshman year the courses I was given, were classics, calculus, which I was totally unprepared for; general chemistry; general biology and French. French was a new language for me. I took 5 years of Spanish and Latin in high school and wanted to try to learn a new language in college. This was a terrible decision for me at that time because I earned a failing grade in beginner's French.

It has been suggested that we should "replace racial quotas with class rank and other criterion because class rank tends to benefit top students at less competitive high schools." I am not sure what was the basis for my selection for admission. What is true is that I did graduate at the top of my high school class. Therefore I would agree with the proposal that selecting students for admission based on their class rank versus just filling racial quotas may prove to be a more acceptable admission strategy for recruiting disadvantaged people of color.

Despite my lack of academic preparation compared to the stalwarts who had attended schools such as the Bronx High School of Science, parochial schools, and private schools such as Packard in Brooklyn, I graduated at the top of my class in Jamaica.

Regarding extracurricular activity, I was an outstanding track star, sang in the school chorus, competed in choral speaking, and just was an all-round excellent student from a small high school in Jamaica.

When the university accepted me for their freshman class of 1966, they took a chance on a student who was very studious and highly motivated. Essentially they "threw me into the pool and said swim."

Based on what I know now as a parent of two girls who went to private colleges and were not on scholarship, the colleges and private high schools that receive federal subsidies must have 10 percent minority or black Americans in the composition of their students recruited. To fulfill this racial quota, they in the sixties recruited foreign African descendants who were in the top ten of their graduating class. As a beneficiary of the affirmative action process, I was totally oblivious of the fact that I was fulfilling a quota. Most of us were totally ecstatic that we were accepted to a prestigious school in the United States of America. My motivation to excel was constant. My so-called disadvantage did not reduce my drive to perform. I was driven by the fact that I left home where I was nurtured by a very spiritual, educated mother who emphasized certain values. One was the importance of what she called "get that little piece of paper." Secondly, my mother always said, "When you have education no one can take it from you. It makes you independent and self-sufficient. If you get married and your husband does not treat you well, you can always leave. You do not have to depend on anyone to take care of you." Having an education was of primary importance in her book. Mom never suggested the kind of profession we as girls should choose since we were three girls. She just wanted us to get an education.

Stereotypic Remarks Concerning Affirmative Action

The allegations made by Stewart Taylor—"The strongest black students know they needn't work as hard as Asians."

Also that "affirmative action is a disincentive to working hard"— this is so far from the truth. I remember in my graduate-school years at the university, I took a course taught by the head of our research laboratory, Dr. Albert Snodon. Whoever excelled in this course was deemed qualified to be a member of this nationally famous hematology research program. I got the highest grade in this course when I took it. Was this because Dr. Snodon liked me and felt sorry for me and gave me the highest grade? Hell no! I worked my butt off to prove that I was just as good as all the others there, the majority of whom were Caucasian students.

In my undergraduate years also at the university, I took mammalian anatomy and got the highest grade. The next semester, Dr. Crossman, who was a dean of the school, invited me to be his teaching assistant. I became the first undergraduate to be hired as a teaching assistant in the biology department. Were they trying to score a point by hiring an African descendant? I don't think so. I worked hard and proved again that I was just as able to compete and excel despite my disadvantage of having to work full-time and go to school full-time.

The assumptions made by Stewart Taylor are similar to one made by a Caucasian female parent at my daughter's high school. My daughter

Michelle was always at the top of her class. She graduated valedictorian and was accepted by all the Ivy League colleges.

This parent said this: "Michelle does not have to worry about being accepted to any of the Ivys because she will be an affirmative action student." Now Michelle was not at the top of her class at an all-black private school. She attended a predominantly white high school with the 10 percent black student population. She competed against majority white students, outperformed them in all her subjects for all the years she attended from grades one through twelve. Why did this parent make the assessment that Michelle would be filling an affirmative action quota? Michelle was not the only African American who attended this school and performed outstandingly. Of course the argument could be made that they did fill the quota of 10 percent of this predominantly white private school. However, the black students who attended came from very supportive families who had high expectations and invested in the lives of their children.

When asked the question "Why did you choose to do medicine?" Michelle would answer, "My mother is a research scientist, and she would take me to her laboratory from the time I was in elementary school so I could watch her work." The truth is that whenever I got up to work in the early morning at about 2:00 a.m., Michelle would be sitting beside me with her pen and paper. I was her best role model.

Most of the students from families with all four grandparents who were born into socially disadvantaged African American communities do not have this kind of role model. Nor do they have these kinds of expectations put upon them either in the schools or in the families. I have African American friends who have said to me, "I wish that my parents had demanded more from me. I was very smart in school, but they had no real expectations for me to excel."

My nephew was an athlete at a school in Florida. He told his coach that he wanted to be a doctor. The coach responded, "I have never had an athlete on my team who became a doctor." My nephew responded, "Well, you are looking at one." Of course he was able to put things in the right perspective. He had his priorities straight. He eventually quit the team and focused on becoming a doctor. Today he is a successful, highly respected, reputable general surgeon who is a partner in private practice in South Carolina. This is one reason why at the beginning of each semester where I teach, I send a message. That message is no concessions are made for athletes in my class. "Tell the coach that if you miss too many lectures or exams in this course, you will fail this course." I put the coach on notice.

Stuart Taylor Jr. states in his newspaper article that "most African Americans of all income levels have subpar academic performance compared to their white counterparts." I think that this is a horrible generalization that gives credibility to the myth that "white people and Asians have superior intelligence." Given the right nurturing, exposure, and similar opportunities, African Americans do just as well and oftentimes better than their white counterparts.

Many African Americans as well as Caribbeans are the first ones in their family to attend college; they do not have the social connections that the white counterparts have. They do not have access to the networking and alumni connections. Thus it is not as easy to navigate the academic world. These things are important determinants in the academic arena.

I remember when I was in graduate school doing research a young lady came in. Her father was the head of medicine at a prestigious medical school in the Midwest. He was a frequent tennis partner for the head of our research laboratory. Her PhD research project was one where she was assigned to a group of white men. Her success was guaranteed before she even started and she was programmed for success. All she had to do was show up and work.

In the research laboratory where I worked in the 1970s–1980s, none of the black students who obtained their doctorates were recommended for postdoctorate positions. This was not because we were not as proficient as the white students or that we did not do as well. My feeling is that they had done enough for us by allowing us the opportunity to achieve a doctorate and just did not want to take a chance on us by recommending us for another opportunity. Consequently, if any one of us got postdoctoral positions, we had to find them for ourselves.

My Mentor Dr. Joseph Logan (1970)

During my freshman year at the university, I made a lifelong friend who was instrumental in my successful career.

Dr. Joseph Logan, who was assigned to be my academic advisor, sent me a letter inviting me to come to his office and meet with him. As a student from the Caribbean, I did not realize that this was standard practice for the biology department. I went to see Dr. Logan, and this changed my entire course of study.

Dr. Logan was warm, caring, and friendly and seemed genuinely to care about my academic development. He was someone who was able to empathize and understand what I was experiencing as a foreign student in New York City. He encouraged me to keep in constant touch with him and I did. Whenever I met with him he would suggest ways that I should employ to circumvent some of the problems I encountered. Little did I know then that he had a graduate student working in his research laboratory who was also from Jamaica and with whom he had a good working relationship.

In my junior year, I registered for a course called experimental hematology, which Dr. Logan taught. In this course, we were taught how to work with mice. First we had to learn how to handle and care for the mice. Then we were taught special hematological techniques such as bloodletting, how to inject the mice with different drugs, how to make and stain slides, how to identify and count blood cells, and how to analyze our data. This course became very useful when I was ready to do research in hematology.

In addition, I was able to utilize the techniques I learned in experimental hematology to get a weekend job as a technician with a doctor in the nearby community. The doctor utilized my hematological skills and allowed me to do finger sticks on patients. I did all the blood cell counts and staining of slides for his patients.

In the spring of 1970, I graduated from College with a bachelor of arts degree. I got married in June of 1970 and settled down in New York with my new husband, not really knowing what my next step would be.

One day when I returned to campus, while walking down the corridors of the biology department, I encountered the woman who worked for the chairman of the department. She was acquainted with me because of my good fortune of being invited to be a teaching assistant for the former Dean Crossman. It was known to all that I was the first undergraduate to be asked to serve as a teaching assistant.

Ms. Rogers asked, "Pat, what are you planning to do next?" Since I had not applied to medical school as planned, I answered, "I am not really sure, Ms. Rogers."

"Well, how would you like to work for Dr. Ropac as his research technician?"

"I would love that, Ms. Rogers."

"Please stop by the office, and we will get your paperwork started so you can begin as soon as possible," she said.

Within a couple of weeks that summer, I began working for Dr. Ropac and was placed under the supervision of three postdoctoral individuals who were also working in the lab. My responsibility was to care for *Amoeba proteus*. In so doing, I had to feed them with paramecium. I also learned how to take care of drosophila fruit flies.

In the fall of 1970, Dr. Ropac without even asking me recommended me for a full scholarship to attend the Graduate School of Arts and Science. I was admitted to the school without even having to take the Graduate Records Examination. It was based on the recommendation of Dr. Milan Ropac, the head of the biology department. I took my first graduate course in biochemical genetics with Dr. Ropac and got an A grade.

During my time in Dr. Ropac's lab, one of the post docs there offered to be my research project advisor. However, I did not find working with amoeba very interesting and so went back to my old friend Dr. Logan and asked him to admit me as a PhD candidate doing research in hematology.

Of course Dr. Logan's response was, "Pat, there will always be a place in my laboratory for you whenever you are ready." With that welcome, I asked Dr. Ropac to relieve me from doing a research project in his lab. He had no objections and willingly gave me permission to transfer my membership to Dr. Logan's hematology research laboratory.

Upon my arrival, I was assigned to begin working with two of the senior graduate students so that I would become more acquainted with the protocols in the lab. Fortunately as mentioned before, I had taken experimental hematology with Dr. Logan and thus was familiar with many of the research methods. I was now on my way to obtaining a master's degree in biology.

During my first official meeting with the research team, Dr. Logan advised me that they were doing investigations with a new strain of Rauscher Leukemia Virus-A and that they needed me to do my master's project using the electron microscope to demonstrate the presence of the virus in all the organs of the BALB/c mice that were infected with the virus.

I had the good fortune also of taking a course in electron microscopy as an undergraduate student. I learned how to fix and stain tissues, how to section them with a microtome, and also to use the electron microscope under the supervision of Dr. Monroe Yonder. I was very happy to be assigned this project and worked arduously to complete the task.

Dr. Logan announced that he had just obtained a research grant and so he would be able to purchase for me a most coveted diamond knife that I would need to use to successfully obtain sections of tissues from mice infected with the RLV-A virus.

I remember the day when we all gathered as a team around the screen of the electron microscope and how excited we were that I was able to demonstrate the virus in the various tissues. This was a terrific accomplishment. We infected the mice with the virus, and in order to really prove that animals were dying from the infected virus, we had to show the presence of the virus in the tissues.

In June 1972, I was awarded a master of science degree from the Biology Department of the graduate school of the university. One day after I completed my master's thesis I got a call from the registrar's office inquiring whether I was planning to attend the 1972 graduation ceremony. They informed me that I was selected for the high honor of accepting the degree on behalf of all the master's degree students for the class of 1972. I quickly accepted the offer and proudly accepted the degree at the graduation ceremony on behalf of all the graduating class.

Soon after this, Dr. Albert S. Roldon, the chairman of the hematology laboratory at the university, offered me a full-time fellowship to continue my work toward obtaining a PhD degree. I was quite surprised and flattered that I was chosen to receive this great honor. Unfortunately, after a few days of receiving this offer, I was informed that I could not accept this fellowship because I was not a United States citizen. This was very disappointing news for me. With the fellowship, I would be able to continue my research project and be able to complete my doctoral dissertation within the next two years. This was not to be since I was not able to afford the tuition for the next two years of course work.

At this time I began thinking of starting a family. I explained my desire to Dr. Logan, and he gave me permission to take leave from the research laboratory. While relaxing at home one day, I picked up the newspaper and decided that I should try to find a job. I looked in the classified advertisement section of the *New York Times* (that was how it was done back then) and identified a position advertised for a supervisor of special hematology at Mellon Hospital in Manhattan. I called up and made an appointment for an interview. The head of the laboratory was very happy to meet an applicant trained in the Albert S. Roldon hematology laboratory. I was hired immediately.

A few months after being at Mellon Hospital, I became pregnant with my first child. We named the baby in the womb Michelle. Although we did not know the sex of the baby, Michelle is a unisex French name by pronunciation. One had just to change the spelling to agree with the sex of the baby.

My first child, Michelle Marie, was born in November 1974. A few weeks into my pregnancy, I got the opportunity to transfer from clinical hematology at Mellon Hospital to Flower and Fifth Hospital doing research in hematology in the department of medicine. During my employment here, I gained tremendous experience in other hematological techniques and cell biology.

1979–1982

In 1979, the biology department at the university notified me that I had one more year left before my ten-year limit for completing courses for my doctoral degree would expire. It was good that during the time I was employed, I continued to do the course work. I returned to my friend and mentor Dr. Logan and asked permission to return to his lab. Of course he welcomed me with open arms and agreed to help me accomplish my goal as much as possible.

Upon my arrival in the laboratory, I encountered a young graduate student who was—or thought that she was—in control of all the space allocation. She informed me that there was no space available for me to work there. She did allow me to have a chair. I sat in front of a stone workbench and watched her for two weeks. During this time, I also made assessment of the space. I began to realize that much of the space in draws was dead space occupied by a great deal of junk. Day by day, I gradually began to empty the junk from some of the draws and carved out some space for myself.

Another item of concern was the available mice with which my experiments had to be done. The mice we worked with came directly from Connecticut because we were collaborating with a virologist, one Dr. T. Fredberg. He injected the mice with a virus he isolated, and we did the hematological investigations on the mice. The graduate student in question would declare when the mice arrived that she needed a certain amount for her experiments and that there were not enough for me to work with. Things got so bad that my husband and I decided that we would go to Connecticut and get mice from Dr. Fredberg so that I would have mice to do my experiments.

One day while walking down the corridors of the lab, I met an old friend from Dr. Ropac's lab. He enquired about the work I was doing. The tissue culture techniques I was using were similar to those used in his laboratory in Valhalla. I shared with him the difficulties I was encountering, and he suggested that I move my research to his laboratory in Valhalla, Westchester.

John gave me a key to his laboratory and also gave me access to many of the chemicals I needed for my investigations. This was tremendous help for me because at that time, funds for research were low. Time was of the essence, and this offer was greatly appreciated.

With this assistance, I became very focused. I planned my experiments carefully and was determined to accomplish my goal, which was to get the work done within a year. On Fridays, I would prepare the animals that were injected with the virus. Friday nights I transported them to Queens where I lived. They slept in my basement for the night. Early Saturday morning, I would set out on my journey to Valhalla to do the experiments.

My goal was to arrive at the laboratory in Valhalla by 9:00 a.m. I worked nonstop until the wee hours of the evening setting up the tissue culture experiments. Once they were completed, I would leave them to incubate for the week. The following weekend, I would harvest my cultures and collect my data.

When I returned home from Valhalla on a Saturday evening, I ate dinner, took a shower, and then settled down to analyze the data I had collected. Over time, I was able to successfully grow erythroid progenitor cells infected with virus in culture. Nevertheless, I encountered another problem. I needed to show my mentor Dr. Logan the colonies grown in culture.

He was not volunteering to come to Valhalla to see them. Therefore I had to take my cultures from Valhalla to Manhattan to show him. Many times I put the culture dishes on ice and drove them to Manhattan to demonstrate the successful growth. Without fail, the colonies would disintegrate before I arrived at the laboratory in Manhattan. Dr. Logan would say each time to me, "I am sure that you had them, I believe that you had them, but I need to see them."

The solution to my dilemma came one day after I read a journal article published by another scientist regarding the ability to clot methylcellulose. Methylcellulose was the medium in which my cultures were grown. If only I could modify this published technique, I would be able to transport the colonies to Manhattan because the colonies would maintain their integrity. In addition, I would be able to obtain photographs of the colonies, which I would need to include in my thesis.

I worked arduously to accomplish this goal. I tried different combinations of clotting factors along with clotting times and length of time for incubation that would be conducive to the growth of my colonies. In approximately two weeks, I was able to accomplish this. I finally got solid clots that did not dissolve. This allowed me to be able to travel from Valhalla to Manhattan and show my colonies grown in methylcellulose. When Dr. Logan observed my colonies, he was elated and instructed me to begin writing my dissertation.

Writing my thesis was utter torment. It was similar to the period of time that I had assigned myself to study for my qualifying exam for the PhD degree. I put off taking this exam for many years simply because of fear that I would fail. I would listen to stories of other students who took this exam, and the more I listened, the greater was my trepidation. Candidates sitting for this exam were expected to know everything and anything about biology. Of course there were sample exams and also guidelines of various subject areas that were provided. I collected all the recommended texts on various topics. I borrowed notes from former students and proceeded to submerge myself into the quagmire of information, hoping to be prepared for this overwhelming task.

One friend of mine gave me some very good advice. She said, "Tell all your friends and acquaintances that you are going to take this examination. This will make it almost impossible for you to cop out." I took this advice and it worked.

I gave myself one month to study for this exam. During this month, I did not leave my house. I slept, woke up, studied and slept, woke up and studied again. I would peer out the window during my study breaks. At this time, my mother catered to my every need.

One week before my exam, my mind went blank. I could not remember anything that I studied previously. This was a real predicament. I prayed earnestly to God for help. The answer to my prayer was that I should prepare questions from various concentration areas. This I did and went to the exam. The examination questions were very similar to those that I prepared, and I was successful in the examination.

Frequently when I was writing my dissertation, I had an intense desire to quit, give it all up, and put it in the garbage. My Christian friends were a real tower of strength to me at that time. I remember what my friend Doreen said to me: "The Lord has not taken you this far to desert you. He certainly is not going to allow you to fail. He will be faithful to see you through to the end." My mother also encouraged me daily to press on and not give up. Eventually, I was successful in completing my writing.

When it was time to defend my thesis, I became fearful again. Then one of my friends in graduate school said, "Do not be afraid. Remember that you know more about your work than any one of the members on your committee." This was very reassuring. I pressed on and finally defended my thesis in May 1981 and was awarded my doctoral degree from the biology department at the Graduate School of Arts and Science at the university.

Soon after the completion of my degree, I found an advertisement in the *New York Times* (since that was how it was done in the 1980s) for a tenure track position in the biology department at one of the universities of New York. Although I was trained as a research scientist and loved working in the research laboratory, I was faced with the reality that I needed to earn "hard money" and not have to be dependent on grant funding.

I submitted my application and was invited to an interview by the search committee. September 1982 I was invited to join the faculty of the biology department as an assistant professor.

1982

I received a letter of appointment from the president of the college stating that I was appointed assistant professor of biology and that my employment would be effective as of September 1982.

A week before the first day of class, I reported to the chairman of the natural science and mathematics division for my working assignment. He stated that he wanted me to become the coordinator of the pre-professional committee and also the premedical advisor. These assignments would be in addition to my regular teaching load. I was assigned three biology courses, two introduction to biology courses, and also general biology. Although the chairman was reluctant he did give me three hours of release time to do the work of the premedical advisor.

Most of my working experience was as a research scientist in a clinical setting. After being at the college for about a week, I discovered that there had been some turmoil at the college where the president was ousted and that the students during this turmoil had certain demands. One student demand was that they wanted a black female hired. Although I knew nothing about this turmoil, my application was timely, and so I got the job as an assistant professor. What I did not know was that there was an individual who had the job of pre-professional advisor. She left suddenly, and therefore her position was incorporated into my role as a faculty member. Thus I was taking on the responsibility of two individuals.

Despite the fact that I had no experience as a pre-professional advisor and very little experience as a teacher, I was ready for the challenge. I remember in the interview that I had with the search committee they asked the question, "What do you think that you have to offer our students here at the college?" My answer was, "I came to America as a foreign student and had to struggle all throughout my years as a student. I worked full-time and went to school full-time, and so I know from personal experience what it is to struggle and to try to achieve."

I remember always the night before I went for this interview that I was at my father-in-law's house. I expressed my reservation about working in Brooklyn in the inner city in Crown Heights. My father-in-law said to me, "Remember diamonds are made in the rough. To get diamonds, you have to dig for them. Go there and dig for the diamonds." This advice kept resonating in my ears and mind.

Pre-professional Advisor 1982–1992

Since I had absolutely no experience serving as the pre-professional advisor and since the person who served in that capacity in the department left, I decided to get help.

I called one by one the dean of admissions at the various medical schools and introduced myself as "the new one on the block" and that I needed help. Everyone was willing to help. One dean in particular invited me to come and visit so he could show me what the role of the premedical advisor was and how I was expected to prepare the student applicant files for admission.

In 1982 there was a group of students predominantly from the Caribbean islands who desperately wanted to go to medical or dental school. It seemed that they were being put off by the previous advisor. Since I was now located in that office, they just assumed I was there to help. We had meetings weekly with these students to ensure them that help was on the way.

One of the students at that time was a young lady who was an alumna of the college. She attended Columbia University Graduate School of Social Work and decided that she wanted to go to medical school. She returned to the college to take the prerequisite courses and thus was in my general biology class. This young lady listened to the advice I gave. She came to me on a weekly basis to prepare her file for admission. Today she tells the story saying, "When I returned to the college, I was advised that I was not a good candidate for medical school and was constantly discouraged from applying. When I met Dr.

Ferdinand, she had a positive attitude, encouraged me and believed in me."

This young lady applied to the University of Buffalo and was accepted. She was a single parent, and so she took her son to Buffalo with her. She successfully completed her medical degree, and today she is a very successful doctor in private practice in downtown Brooklyn.

During my tenure as the premedical advisor, I realized that many (not all) students coming from the public schools in New York City have very little confidence in their ability to achieve in science. The expectations for them are very low. They do not know how to struggle.

In addition to my job of preparing their files for admission, I became a role model, passing on many of the words of encouraging sayings I got from my mentors, the chief of them being my mother. She would say to me things like "If you want to succeed, you must burn the midnight oil—hard work never killed anyone, and so you have to press on," and of course she gave me a Bible verse that I hold dear and that I passed on to my own children, which is, "I can do all things through Christ, who strengthens me."

Another thing that I did as premedical advisor was to develop a working relationship with the various deans by inviting them to come and visit the college and meet with the students there.

It was then that their eyes were opened to the kinds of students that we had. These were students with great enthusiasm and motivation and who needed help to access the system.

In addition to having them come to the college, colleagues of mine and I would visit the various medical schools with the intention of partnering with them to help these students.

My first year as the premedical advisor, I succeeded in getting three students accepted into medical school. During my tenure as the advisor, I placed a minimum of fifteen students into medical and dental schools. All of these students have completed their training and are successful practicing physicians in the different states of the United States.

Juggling My Role in Academia with Motherhood

In 1983, a year after I joined the faculty at the college, I discovered that I was two months pregnant with my second child, Andree Louise. She was born January 17, 1984. I stayed home with her for six months before returning to work. This was a real pleasure for me because when my first child, Michelle, was born, I returned to work six weeks after she was born. At that time in 1974, I was just beginning my career as a research scientist and was determined to take advantage of all the opportunities available. My director at that time was a female doctor from India. She thought that six weeks was too long because she said, "Women in the East return the next day to work after their baby is born." Since I was not a woman living in the East, I insisted on taking a minimum of six weeks off.

The time spent at home with Andree was most enjoyable. Soon after my return to work in the biology department at the college, I realized that raising two children as a non-tenured faculty member would be an uphill struggle. The Natural Science Department had a minimum of three women and was composed of predominantly male faculty.

I learned very early in my research career at the various hospitals that women in a man's world cannot expect any compassion or special favors from their male colleagues. The demands of the job are the same, and why shouldn't they be?. The reality then was that many of my male colleagues had the wives at home taking care of the children. Consequently, there was little consideration given to the time departmental meetings were scheduled. My husband worked in Manhattan, and my daughter went to school in Long Island, so I would have to always be concerned about going home early to relieve the babysitter or coming in late because the babysitter did not show up for work.

Sometimes I would have to wrap up the baby at the last minute and take her to my mother-in-law in Brooklyn because the babysitter did not show up for work on a Monday morning. She lived on the sixth floor of an apartment building, which had no elevators. I had to make my way up six flights of stairs with the baby. On a cold snowy day it was the baby along with the stroller. On one occasion when I had a nine o' clock class, I had to take her into the office and hand her to the secretary of the department. She would hold the baby until my early class ended. To solve the unpredictable schedule of a babysitter, I finally decided to hire a live-in nanny, and this really helped.

Tenure Application

The requirements for obtaining tenure at the college were quite challenging. Faculty are evaluated in nine areas: administration, teaching, college-wide committees, departmental committees, community service, student service, and research and publication.

To accomplish this goal, one has to commit to intense interaction with other members of the college. This level of interaction is different from that of being a student. To succeed I needed to solicit advice and support of those senior faculty and administrators who had gone before.

One of my friends, who was a director of Cooperative education at the college, advised that I should identify people who could serve as my mentors. This I did. Another senior faculty advised, "Pretend that you are coming up for tenure at Harvard. Prepare your file accordingly. Your file should reflect excellence in all nine areas."

Another friend and faculty member shared her file with me so that I could see the format for presentation. Others invited me to sit on committees that they chaired so that I would have the opportunity to produce evidence of my involvement. When I came up for tenure, I was involved as a member of fifteen different committees.

In addition to my teaching load and service as the pre-professional advisor, I also had to engage in research without the help of a technician. This was a challenging journey for me. My daughter Michelle was already twelve years old, in junior high school, and needed my attention when I got home. Then there was the second girl, Andree Louise, who was born two years after I began working at the college. The wonderful thing about this was the fact that I had a very supportive husband who was totally involved in our lives. We had our church friends, who supported us spiritually and emotionally. Then there was the support from my mother, who would come to visit in the summers and help so that I could be totally involved in my laboratory research.

The time allotted to fulfill the requirements for application for tenure was five years. At the end of five years, I had to prepare files that would provide evidence of my total involvement. My husband, who is a perfectionist in making graphs and preparing documents, worked laboriously to assist me. We put the original documents into spiral binders and sent them off to the printers for reproduction.

The final documents first were presented to the departmental Personnel, Management, and Budget Committee (PMB) for them to vote on the files. Then they were forwarded to the tenure committee. From the tenure committee, the files were sent to the college-wide (PMB) committee. Here all the chairpersons from all the various departments of the college had an opportunity to inspect, review, and approve or disapprove the granting of tenure.

I was successful in the process and was granted tenure in 1987.

In 1992, I became the first female person of color to be the head of the Natural Science and Mathematics Department. Two years later, I applied for the appointment to full professor and was successful.

I now spend my time mentoring students, encouraging and challenging them to reach for the stars, have high expectations of themselves and not to be satisfied with mediocrity.

I also see myself as a mentor and advocate for younger African American faculty in the department.

My Reflections on God

There is a song that says "When I look back over my life and I think things over; I can truly say that I've been blessed; I have a testimony." My testimony is also expressed in this song and in certain verses from the bible.

Psalm 118: verse 7 "He taketh my part with them that help me."

It was my profound faith in God that enabled me to leave the shores of the island of Jamaica to come to the United States to attend one of the universities in the city, not knowing how I was going to make it financially.

In the book of Hebrews chapter 11:6–9, it says,

> But without faith it is impossible to be well pleasing to Him, for he who comes forward to God must believe that he is and that He is a rewarder of those who diligently seek Him.

> By faith Noah, having been divinely instructed concerning things not yet seen and being moved by pious fear, prepared an ark for the salvation of his house, through which he condemned the world, and became heir of the righteousness which is according to faith.

> By faith Abraham, being called, obeyed to go out unto a place which he was to receive as an inheritance; and he went out, not knowing where he was going.

> By faith he dwelt as a foreigner in the land of promise as
> in a foreign land, making his home in tents with Isaac
> and Jacob.

My first opportunity came when I was accepted as a student to attend one of the largest private universities in the United States. I certainly was not accepted based on my scholastic aptitude test scores. I did not receive an academic scholarship and thus had absolutely no idea of how I was going to be able to pay tuition. I came and trusted that God would help me to find a way.

After I completed my undergraduate studies, I was clueless as to what I would do next since I did not apply to medical school or graduate school. People intervened on my behalf, and based on my performance as an undergraduate, I received help.

God has a way of placing people in your life to help and to guide you. Ms. Rogers, the secretary of the biology department, offered me the opportunity to work in the research lab for the head of the biology department, Dr. Ropac. Soon after I began there, Dr. Ropac, seeing my aptitude, signed me up for graduate school. There in the lab, I met and became friends with Dr. John Mutton, who later became a collaborator in my PhD project. Then there was Dr. Anne Hamburger, who supported and encouraged me in all my endeavors.

My church friends were a tremendous source of encouragement and inspiration. The messages that I heard when I attended weekly Sunday meetings were a source of inspiration. One of the messages I heard that helped me tremendously was one concerning Moses, a character in the Bible.

Moses was called by God to lead the children of Israel out of Egypt into the wilderness. Moses was raised in Pharaoh's palace. He forsook the privileges and comforts of the palace and stepped out not relying on his own strength. God promised Moses that he would be with him.

He promised to be to him the great "I am," meaning he would be to him whatever he needed. As Moses and the children of Israel journeyed through the wilderness, they had to depend on God completely for food, which was daily manna from above, and for guidance as they were led by a pillar of clouds by day and a ball of fire by night.

It was much the same for me as I undertook my educational pursuits as a graduate student. During my four years as an undergraduate, I had to work full-time in the evenings from 5:00 p.m. to 11:00 p.m. I worked in Greenwich Village in downtown Manhattan. I lived in Queens on the south side of Long Island. After work at night, I would travel by subway from West Fourth Street in Manhattan to the end of the line in Jamaica Queens. Then I would have to wait for at least fifteen to twenty minutes for the bus, which took me on a forty-five-minute ride to my destination.

When I disembarked, I then had to walk for about five blocks to my place of residence in the dark. Often I would walk along with strangers, who insisted on relating dangerous events that had happened recently. I really could not afford to listen to these stories. I just lifted my thoughts to God and asked for protection. I had a goal, and if I had to accomplish my goal of completing my four-year study as an undergraduate, I could not focus on the dangers of traveling at night.

I reflected on this verse in Galatians: "The mind stayed on the Spirit is Life and Peace." I needed and still need this peace, which only God can abundantly supply.

There are many instances of how God helped me during these for years as an undergraduate. I had friends who were faithful to take care of my spiritual as well as physical needs. Mine was a journey in faith. God was faithful to carry me through. I believe that this person we call God is the Creator of the universe and is in control of everything. This Creator takes care of the birds of the air and the lilies of the fields and is concerned about each one of us.

My Husband, Donald Ferdinand

Another portion of my accomplishments belong to this man. I met him in 1968 while working at the Fifth Avenue cinema in the West Village. One day while I was sitting in the box office doing my homework assignment for chemistry, I heard a voice (since my head was down) saying, "So you have come back."

I did not recognize the voice nor did I understand the question. I looked up and asked, "What do you mean?"

"Well, I noticed that you were away this past week and wondered where you were," he said.

I explained that I had just returned to Jamaica for a short vacation.

He explained that he worked next door to the cinema and that he passed by the cashier's box every evening after work. After this, he would stop by the box to talk every evening after work. I discovered that he was from the island of Haiti and that he was fluent in French. I told him that I had failed French in my freshman year, and so he began to help me with my conversation in French while I helped him with his English since he had recently come to the United States.

Our meetings at the cashier box continued until he began asking me if I would go out with him after work for dinner. Normally when I was approached for a date by a stranger, I would give the excuse that I had to work late and so was unavailable. Furthermore, "I have to study after I get home from work, so I will not be available," I would say.

These excuses did not work because he was very persistent. He would counter my excuses every time with a solution to the problem I presented. He insisted that on Fridays after work, he would meet me for dinner, and after dinner, he would accompany me home.

"But I have to be home at a certain time," I said. He countered with, "I promise that if you go out with me, I will be sure to take you home to Queens safely and on time." I agreed to go out with him.

Our Friday night dates were in the West Village, where we would visit different ethnic restaurants. If we went to a Spanish restaurant, we would converse in Spanish because we were both conversant in that language. When we visited a French restaurant, we spoke in French. My ability to converse in French was limited, and so he became the teacher and I the student.

These Friday night excursions continued until I began to look forward to this time of recreation, which I probably needed after a demanding and stressful week at school. My newfound friend turned out to be a very caring and considerate individual. He was concerned about my very demanding schedule and played a tremendous role in helping me cope.

After a year of dating, he proposed, and we were married June 1970 soon after I graduated from college. Immediately after I enrolled in graduate school. My new husband was just as supportive as he had been while we were dating.

Two years after we were married, I was ready to graduate from the Graduate School of Arts and Science with a master's degree in biology.

What I Believe

Our society has been doing something special against the negro for hundreds of years. How then can he be absorbed into the mainstream of American life if we do not do something special for him now, in order to balance the equation and equip him to compete on a just and equal basis.

—Martin Luther King

The questions I ask is, Why should the affirmative action law that was designed for descendants of slaves, the oppressed, children of single family homes, and children of the inner city be allowed to stand?

Why should they have access into a world where the playing field is not level, where the education system is not equal, into a world where they will be continually be devalued?

President Lyndon B. Johnson said, "Freedom is not enough. You do not take a person who for years has been hobbled by chains and liberate him, bring him up to the starting line of a race, and then say, 'You are free to compete with all the others.'"

Claude M. Steele cites research done at a prestigious university where only 18 percent of black students have grade averages of B or above as compared with 64 percent of their white counterparts."

Bear in mind that segregation and mistreatment of black Americans took place not long ago and is still taking place in America. Therefore I believe it is necessary to give the process of affirmative action a chance to work for those for whom it was designed.

One prestigious medical school made a commitment in the 1990s to ensure that their first-year medical school class consisted of 20 percent women and 10 percent of those women would be black women. Of course it is true that all these black women were from better-off homes where at least one parent was an educated professional and also that these women, including my daughter, were from the top ten of their graduating high school class.

The point also needs to be made that some, including my daughter, attended private schools where the majority of their class was white. They earned higher grades than their white or Asian classmates. They were not given these grades because of affirmative action. Nor were they accepted into the Ivys because of affirmative action. Many were competitive and desirable candidates to all the Ivys in the United States.

However, this commitment was a challenge to these women in a majority Ivy League environment. They lived together, studied together, and supported each other in this very competitive majority environment. They all graduated with shining colors and are today successful doctors.

As the years roll on, this 20/10 percent minority will go out and serve as role models for other women of color, sending the message that it is possible to succeed in the sciences. They will be able to open doors of opportunities for other African Americans.

As these advantages increase for people of color, whether earned or because of affirmative-action opportunity, the socially and economically disadvantaged will be able to take advantage of the educational opportunities offered. These successful black Americans will be able to perpetuate and sustain certain values that are necessary for success. Young black Americans will be able to rise to the expectations critical for the higher educational standards.

One African American doctor who came to speak to my students while I was the premedical advisor said this, "I was one of twelve children who grew up on welfare. I understand that children from the inner city in such a plight do not have as their priority the desire to succeed and earn high grades in school. Their daily priority or preoccupation is where or when will I get my next meal, where will I sleep tonight, what clothes do I have to wear to school?"

Many of these students because of their living conditions have been exposed to sexual and physical abuse. They themselves are single parents. My experience of students at the college where I am a professor is that many of these single-parent students have more than one child and are trying to get back on track. Many have to miss classes when the child is sick, some are dealing with fathers who are not paying child support and so they are in and out of court, and others are dealing with eviction from their place of residence because they cannot pay the rent.

It is understandable why the attrition rate is high for many African American students trying to get an education. Therefore the affirmative action laws should be allowed to work more to facilitate socially and economically disadvantaged African Americans.

Should foreign students of color be benefactors of this law? I say yes because many foreign students like myself from different backgrounds with different skills and values that they bring are able to enhance the playing field.

The question to be asked is this; Do Caribbean and African students have different social values that cause them to be chosen over African American students when affirmative action is *enforced*?

The institution of slavery had a profound effect on the structure of the black family in America as compared to that which occurred in the Caribbean Islands. One reason for this is that most of the colonizers (such as the British, French, Spaniards, and Dutch) after slavery was abolished left the island. They also encouraged the islanders to be educated and to develop in the absence of continued suppression, whereas the oppressors in America never left. Many of the ills of slavery were dealt with by putting a Band-Aid over the wrongs.

One consequence of slavery in America was the emergence of the "single-mother family." White males exploited the female slaves. Slave families were broken up by the sale of the husband and the father. Decades after slavery, single-mother families continued to exist for a variety of reasons.

Specific government policies encouraged the break-up of the slave families. For example, up until the late 1960s, "man in the house" welfare rules denied aid to a mother who was associated with a man.

Although today black American families have the same legal status as white families, the persistence of racism often leaves black families subject to many of the same pressures that they were forced to cope with during slavery. There were no such regulations in the Caribbean islands when I was growing up. First, we did not and still do not have such welfare laws. The existence of the nuclear family was encouraged. The family unit where it existed was strong with many family values passed down from parents and grandparents to the children. It cannot be denied that there are single mothers with single family homes raising what Jamaicans called illegitimate children similar to single families in America.

To be called illegitimate was not something to be proud of. Women had children oftentimes so that they could get support from the more privileged fathers. This did not negate the fact that these illegitimate children had access to education. Some attended the best schools. To be illegitimate did not mean that you were necessarily poor or of a low class.

Black women in America keeping single-family homes were called matriarchs. Ironically, the mothers of families in Jamaica were and still are considered the matriarchs of the family. This is a very important and complimentary status to delegate to a mother. My mother, when she was alive, was the proud matriarch of our family. As such, she taught us our family values. One of the most important values for my mother, who was an elementary-school teacher, was education. She never emphasized the importance of having wealth or going after money. She insisted that we had to "get that little piece of paper." Meaning that we had to go to school and to college and become educated so that we could be independent and assertive women not depending on a man for support. She also taught us to be honest and to work hard and study hard. My mother's favorite saying was, "By the sweat of your brow you shall eat bread." Another one was "If you want good, your nose will have to run." She taught us to have a strong faith in God. She taught us Bible verses such as "I can do all things through Christ who strengthens me." My mother used the prayers sent to her by Unity School of Christianity. She would teach us some of these prayers so we could recite them when we went to school. One of these prayers was related to our studying and went like this: "The all-knowing mind of God is in me. I think clearly and remember what I learn." My mother encouraged us to pray daily. I remember having to kneel down by the bedside with my mother to pray every morning and night before we went to bed.

I am sure that many black American families, especially those in the South, did these kinds of things. The black church was and still is a very important function in the African American community.

In America, mothers had to teach their children to value themselves in a society whose message was that they were not valued and had no value. The daily challenge was to instill values of pride and self-esteem.

This was not as difficult a task in the islands despite the poverty and social class structure that existed because children were not constantly devalued by the portrayal of negative images as it exists for black people in the American society. These negative images are spoken and implied in advertising, on television, in magazines, and in the department stores. President Clinton said, "Crime has a black face in America." If crime is associated with having a black face, why would anyone want to be associated with that kind of image? Consequently among African Americans, there is a lot of self-hatred, people with low self-esteem and low self-worth.

In America, there are not many types of role models for children to emulate. A great deal of importance is placed on aspiring to be a sports star or to be a movie or music sensation. When I was growing up in Jamaica, we had no television on the island. We knew that to be important, one had to be educated. That was our gateway to fame and fortune. At least that was what we were taught. Although Jamaica is a multiracial society, the predominant race is black, so we were accustomed to seeing successful black people, people who owned and sailed boats, black people living in palatial dwellings, black people who were leaders of our country. Whereas in America, 2009 was the first time a black man and his family were elected to the office of the presidency. Now the Congress is determined "by any means possible he should not be allowed to succeed."

The school system was different. We were not confined to neighborhood schools. If you did not like the school in the neighborhood you lived in and you were able to take a bus, walk, or drive, you were free to attend the school of your choice as long as you were able to pass the admission test. Poor blacks from the slums (because that's how we called it) had a ticket out of their social plight. If they sat for the common entrance exam and obtained a passing grade, they would gain acceptance to any of the best high schools in Jamaica.

Class prejudice was the nemesis of the Caribbean islands. The Europeans left this with us. They divided the people into social classes. Thus in Jamaica, upward social mobility was gained not solely by gaining riches but by becoming educated.

Education was not always available for the poorer class because most of the high schools were privately owned. The University of the West Indies was not easily accessible. Therefore those who were poor and could not pass the government-aided scholarship could not achieve an education. Poverty and class prejudice were the main limiting factors in social mobility.

The islands also had their share of color prejudice. It was not black versus white supremacy. Ours was a matter of complexion and quality of hair. Those individuals who had the light complexion and hair that was not coarsely textured had more privileges than the darker skin people with more African features.

The lighter-skin individuals (mixed) were frequently from the upper class. They had more of the wealth and therefore more access to education in Jamaica. Thus there are many problems in Jamaica that mirror the racial problems in America.

Me in my office (at work)

Me as a High school girl in Jamaica

Washington Square Park, 1968

Berkley California 1963

My High School Graduation in Jamaica WI

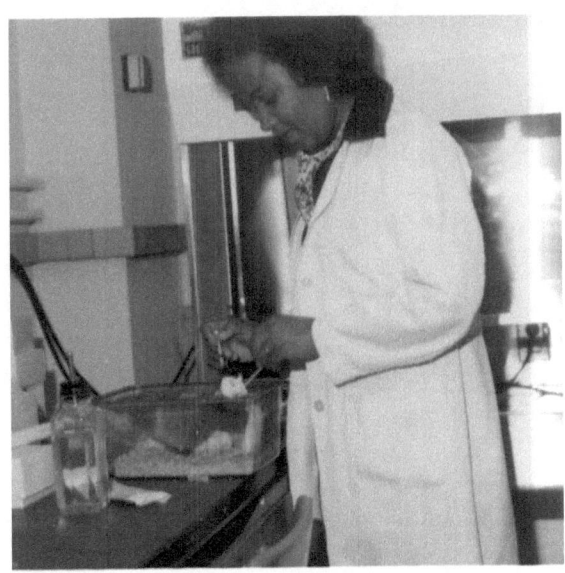

Me in the laboratory

My husband Donald and I

My Mother-My Greatest Teacher, Eglantine M. Gordon

Index

W

West Village, 25, 54-55
Whensaw, Myron, 27
Woodsley Primary School, 12

Y

Yonder, Monroe, 37

Z

Zeke, 7-8

www.ingramcontent.com/pod-product-compliance
Lightning Source LLC
Chambersburg PA
CBHW030523290526
45786CB00004B/1587